FOLLOW™
~~LEADER~~ship
A Next Up Mentality

Nelson J. Estrada

Copyright © 2022 Nelson Estrada Communications
ISBN:
Printed in the United States of America | All Rights Reserved. No part of this publication may be reproduced, stored in a retrieval system, or transmitted in any form by any means – electronic, mechanical, photocopying, recording, or otherwise – without prior written consent.

DEDICATION

This book is dedicated to anyone who didn't know what to do with their lives, because someone told them never be a follower; but they didn't feel like a leader. I pray it doesn't take you long to realize all great leaders; need great followers. Thank you to INC.com, HBR.com, Forbes.com and many other S.M.E.'s on this topic and for the endless amounts of excellent professional op-eds. It gives me hope that we may see a shift from following as a sign of weakness to following as a sign of true strength and courage.

FOLLOW™
~~LEADER~~ship
A Next Up Mentality

CONTENTS

	The Beginning	3
1	F.W.I.	Pg 9
2	"Ah, this is so hard for I"	Pg 14
3	The 'Yes' men	Pg 22
4	It wasn't me; it was the one-armed man	Pg 27
5	Thank you to all, and to all a goodnight	Pg 35
6	1+1 is definitely 11	Pg 46
7	Bonnie and Clyde	Pg 55
8	Kendrick Lamar	Pg 61
9	Yoga	Pg 65
10	Old Faithful	Pg 71
11	"The eagle fly's west at dawn"	Pg 75
12	I couldn't do this without you	Pg 79
13	You don't have to be a keynote	Pg 85
14	"Are we there yet"	Pg 91
	Conclusion	Pg 95

FOLLOW™ ~~LEADER~~ship

A Next Up Mentality

ACKNOWLEDGMENTS

I want to first thank my family for being supportive during this process, I only grind it out for you. Secondly, I would like to thank God for allowing me to discover my passion. Thirdly, I would like to thank any and all people who have been under my charge, you make me the leader I am able to be today. Without great followers, I will never be a great leader.

FOLLOW ~~LEADER~~ship™

A Next Up Mentality

The Beginning

For decades there has been a stigma with the term 'follower'. Everyone is told to be a leader. Although leadership is taught, not everyone is a leader. Some people need someone to lead them. Now, I am not in any way referring to following someone or something, blindly. I am referring to aligning and following something or someone that mirrors your values and passion. Someone or something you can get behind and help move the mission forward. I remember as a kid, we all wanted to be captain when picking our basketball team or football team. We wanted to be the leader. The one making decisions and taking the responsibility of the 'win' on our shoulders. The truth is not everyone is built for that. Not everyone has that ability to take on that type of pressure. As a matter of fact, if you were one desperately seeking that captain role, you may want to check your own motives there.

Some people just want to be involved and that is absolutely fine. There is nothing wrong with a great foot soldier. But that is the caveat, just because you are a follower, does not mean you get to walk away from being great. In this book, I am going to talk about what it looks like to be in 'Followship' not leadership. If you know me personally, or read my first book, you will know how much I love leadership. I was built for it. I love the pressure and developing people. In this book, I will be taking a little different approach. I am going to write about the

10 characteristics of a great follower. You will read the term 'Followship' quite a bit. Think of it as the word 'leadership' but for followers.

My hope is that this helps someone do well in second chair or help someone find peace in the workplace not being in charge and following someone that is. Followers have a huge responsibility as well, that responsibility is finding the right leader to follow. We will talk about how to identify that leader and how to follow them to best support them. This is how you add tremendous value as a follower. You support your leader with fervor. I can give you a perfect example of someone who was a follower that added tremendous value to the leader. Ever heard of Nelson Mandela? He was the President of South Africa for a period. He was also the first black Head of State for them. Clearly, a revolutionary. Nelson Mandela served 27 years in prison, and while in prison, he made a tremendous impact. He could not have done that without the support of his follower, Walter Sisulu. Sisulu was considered a mentor to Mandela. But still one of his followers.

He was part of the African National Congress. Although never President of South Africa, he made an impact on the country as a follower. He was so passionate about the movement he and Mandela were pursuing; that he was arrested in 1961 for high treason and acquitted only to be convicted of sabotage 3 years later and sentenced to life imprisonment. In 1989 Sisulu was released after 26 years of imprisonment. He played an enormous impact on the election of President Mandela and helped make history in South Africa. He followed Mandela all the way to prison. Now, in no way am I suggesting you follow someone to prison, but what I am trying to do is paint a vivid picture of what a dedicated follower looks like. If you have a leader with a great cause and mission, that you can bond yourself to, there is nothing wrong with not being in charge. There is now a botanical garden and university named after Walter Sisulu, in his honor.

  Let's look at another follower, Steve Kerr. He was a guard for the Chicago Bulls in the 90's, with teammate Michael Jordan. Steve Kerr is another example of a great follower, becoming a great leader because of it. Steve Kerr's coach was Phil Jackson, an NBA Hall of Fame, legendary coach. Phil Jackson was Steve Kerr's leader. Mr. Jackson gave Mr. Kerr a specific task for his role on the team, it wasn't incredibly fancy, like it is now. It was the boring role in the 90's, to be honest. Steve's role was to hit the 3-ball. We put you in the game when we need a 3, you don't have to do much else, just hit the 3. Now, on Steve Kerr's team is, arguably, the greatest basketball player of all-time. The one and only Michael Jordan. Clearly, everyone on the Bulls were overshadowed by Mr. Jordan. With that being said, Steve Kerr could have easily said "Let the 'greatest' hit the 3".

  Rather than getting his ass on his shoulders and not being happy about being the top dog on the team, he fulfilled his purpose. He knew the assignment. Now, Steve Kerr has championship rings as both a player and a head coach of the Golden State Warriors. Ironically, he has the greatest 3-point shooter of all-time on his team. He is leading the guy who can take the mission and vision of the 3-ball from being boring in basketball, to the next level (which has been fulfilled). Mr. Sisulu wasn't after the title of President of South Africa. Steve Kerr wasn't after becoming a hall of fame basketball coach like his former coach. But here they are. Why? Because they were great followers.

This isn't a book about how to be a great follower to be a great leader (even though that is the exact path of a great leader), this is about being a great follower and being happy about that. Think about followship like your first dance at your wedding reception. You are both decent dancers, who can keep your rhythm. Now, imagine you both had headphones on. You are listening to one song and your spouse is listening to another. The idea is to dance together to the same tune. Given that neither one of you know what song you're listening to, the chances of this going well is unlikely. Followship is the same way.

You and your leader must be on the same song, going to the same tune and on the same rhythm. In order to do that, followers must be in a consistent communication and flow with their leader. That is why your role is so important as the follower. Your leader is unsuccessful with poor followers. Followship is not a negative. It's a huge positive. Followers help change the world. Followship still requires risk, followship still requires discipline. It is not free of stress, but it is rewarding to know you helped someone succeed. You don't follow for recognition of your commitment; you follow because you believe in the vision, just as much as the leader; and believe the person you are following can help achieve said mission. Followship is admirable. Followship is courageous and hard to do. Our flesh, our ego and pride can get in the way of us doing tremendous things as a follower. After all it is called Batman and Robin. Not Robin and Batman. But Robin saved Batman's behind a few times. He never got a blockbuster movie, but he was remembered and made an impact. Can you ignore the shining lights and notoriety; to make a great impact and move in your calling as a follower? Let's dive in!

F.W.I.

A follower isn't necessarily just someone who simply is committed to someone or something that shares like-minded interests and/or principles. Sometimes a follower has influence. The reason they choose to humbly follow someone or something, is for the greater cause. They believe that person or group can carry the cause or principles further than they could from their God-given anointing or influence. That does not mean they don't possess influence. As an example. Barack Obama was the 44th President of the United States of America. Barack Obama won the "popular" vote and the necessary electoral votes to become the President, twice. His running mate was Joseph Biden. A likeable Vice-President with an extensive political history.

He had influence in D.C. More than Barack Obama at the time Barack ran for President, however, Joseph Biden accepted his offer to be Vice-President because he felt Barack Obama could carry those shared ideals further than he could. Otherwise, he could've ran on his own. 12 years later, Joseph Biden became the 46th President of the United States of America. He sustained enough political influence in his vice-presidency to run for President and win. Now, whether you voted for him or not, doesn't really matter. What matters here is the influence he had to win. Joe Biden was a follower of Barack Obama and now in the history books as both a Vice-President and President of the United States of America. A follower with influence or an 'FWI' is a powerful position. An FWI gets the opportunity to absorb so much knowledge and experience, while still making an impact in the same world as the leader. Being an FWI is incredible. I believe every great leader was an FWI. Now, being an FWI does not guarantee you to be a great leader. There are other factors to that you can read in my 1st book; "Leading from the Roots: 11 Characteristics of a Great Leader". I, myself have been an FWI, and I have both succeeded and failed at it (by some standards). Let me share a story of my failure as an FWI, where I learned what it meant to be a great follower.

I was part of a church in my hometown, that I was committed to. I attended for 11 years and was heavily planted and serving in my church. Community events, Conferences, Youth Ministry, even their Bible College. I felt jolted internally to become a pastor (so I thought). Biblically speaking, before pursuing this passion, you are to get the blessing from your current pastor and spiritual leader. Instead of seeking his blessing, I announced I was going to plant a church. I was beyond excited and thought I was carrying on the mission of the local church.

When I reached out to my pastor, he sent, what I felt was a scathing email. He essentially shattered my self-esteem and told me I wasn't built for it. Now, could his approach have been better? Sure! Does that matter now? No. It was a teaching moment for me. The first teaching moment is that I should've invested more time in being around him and seeing what his world was like. I should've told him my goal and see if he was willing to mentor me or guide me along the process. Some reading this may disagree and that is ok. In my heart, I know he was right to correct me, I just didn't like to hear it at the time. I knew better. My ego just couldn't accept it. I say all this to say, I had the influence to do it and I did it.

We launched and it was an interesting season of my life. I learned a lot about character, discipline, and leading people. In my eyes, he is still a stellar leader. All leaders have moments that could've been handled better, no one is perfect. I share this story with partial detail to help you avoid making the same mistake I made, not following a great leader to the end. If it is your defined season to branch out on your own, fantastic! But make sure your current leader is a part of the process. They are where they are for a reason! Leadership is hard in and of itself, it is even harder when you have rogue follower with influence. It can actually be catastrophic. Being a follower is great. It is a fun season of life when you are following the right leader.

However, moving out from under their influence, can potentially be detrimental to your own success as a leader. In the spiritual world, we call that favor. But this isn't a spiritual book. This is a book about being a great follower. I want to remove the stigma of what it means to be a follower. There is NOTHING wrong with being a follower. Not everyone is meant to lead, and some remove themselves from under the protective umbrella of their current leaders influence too fast. It's ok to follow someone your entire life but trust your leader when they say you aren't ready OR that you ARE ready. Both are hard pills to swallow sometimes. Being a leader isn't easy, it's pretty scary at times.

Don't be so quick to take control of the helm, sometimes you haven't spent enough time on a rough sea. However, do not be afraid to fail. Failure is how you learn. Let's dive into what it means to be a great follower. In this book, I am going to present to you 13 characteristics of a great follower. You may think of more to add, and that is fine. But just like my last book, you cannot remove any of these 13 and still be considered great. Are you ready to grow as a follower and prepare yourself for a successful future as a great leader or sustain your greatness as a follower? Let's go!

"Ah, this is so hard for I"

One of my favorite t.v. shows of all-time is *Will & Grace*. A hilarious slapstick comedy about two best friends from NY, who live in a nice little apartment together. The male best friend is *Will*, he is a gay corporate attorney. His best friend is *Grace*, she once dated *Will* and was in love with him in college, where he decided to "come out" to her. They have two other close friends they consistently spend time with, *Karen* and *Jack*. *Karen* is a wealthy alcoholic gold-digger who works for *Grace*, as her assistant, just to do it. *Jack* is the hilariously flamboyant friend that helped *Will* come out and is also gay. He is an aspiring, nurse, and Actor, who really can't find what he wants to do in life. So, he lives life aimlessly off *Will's* credit cards. He is self-sabotaging and literally one of the funniest characters I have ever seen on a t.v. show. With that being said, in a particular episode, *Jack* is struggling trying to think of something and he says; "Ah, this is so hard for I". Completely struggling with Critical thinking and apparently, English.

As a leader, one of the greatest feelings is to go to a follower of yours and provide a goal for them to accomplish. A task that no matter the size, will help achieve the mission or vision. Then only have to go back to check on progress, not walk them through step-by-step on how to do it. That is called delegation, that is what leaders do. They delegate. In order for you to be a great follower, you must be an independent, critical thinker. Critical thinking is about examination. What I mean by that is, examining the issue or challenge in front of you.

Your leader gives you a task. You do not have all the answers, but they did communicate what they are expecting the end-result to look like…because you asked the appropriate questions. That is another key part to critical thinking, asking the right questions. But let's get back to the examining. Prior to the incredible advancement in modern technology, doctors were forced to be heavy critical thinkers. Let me be clear, I believe they still are to this day; however, modern technology has taken quite a load off their plates. We as patients would visit our primary care doctor with a concern, they would ask some probing question to help assess their diagnosis, based on their educated guess, they would diagnose their patients.

Now, there has been such an advancement in modern day technology and medicine, they order labs and exams to help them come to a more succinct and confident diagnosis. Followers don't always have that luxury. So, they must think critically. They ask themselves questions like; "What is my leader trying to say here?", "What did she mean by 'x,y,z'?"

By becoming a critical thinker, your leader can begin to trust you and trust you with more responsibility, creating autonomy for yourself. Followers must gather intel to help formulate a decision or direction with the assigned responsibility. Maintaining a sense of autonomy over your work is important in followship. It is about maintaining your time and creating new opportunities and responsibilities for yourself. Critical thinking is not something everyone does, but they are certainly able to do so. Just like common sense is no longer so common. Critical thinking is not a starting point for some people. Part of becoming a critical thinker, as a follower, falls on the leader.

As leaders, we are to involve the follower in planning. That is where you can hear your leader think critically and ask questions that maybe you never would've thought of. I have worked for leaders who I simply wanted to listen to on conference calls because they were brilliant at asking questions. These questions identified critical missing pieces, areas of concern or risk and made everyone in the meeting think differently. That is what a great follower does, they think of things that the leader might not have. It doesn't make the leader any less great or you any greater than the leader, it simply adds value to the mission. That is where your mindset must be. I am not better or less than, I am simply adding value. After all we get paid to add value, not clock-in. Followship is such a critical piece to the success of the leader, that it warranted me writing a book about it. Because if a leader has bad followers, he/she will not be successful.

Of course, a great set of followers, does not guarantee success either, it certainly helps. When it comes to thinking critically, there is a process to it. Michael Tomaszewski wrote in article on <u>zety.com</u> in April of 2021 and he listed 7 steps to Critical Thinking. Here is what he said, first step: 'Identify the problem or question'. Michael is spot on. When faced with a scenario to think critically we must be able to identify what the issue is. Let's go with car problems. We have all had those. Then he says to 'Gather data'. In 2016, Dr. Rafiq Elmansy wrote an article for Designorate.com around the 6 steps for effective critical thinking.

He laid out a framework, if you will, around what it looks like visually to critically think. He stated the six steps were knowledge, comprehension, application, analyze, synthesis and take action. I felt all these steps were very important, but one really stood out to me, that was synthesis. The synthesis stage is where the decision is made. There could be several options to the solution of the matter, but there is a solution at this stage that the follower must be able to identify. Once you identify the solution, you now analyze its potential success at solving the problem. That is what great followers do, they break it down to the finest detail to ensure they are making a great decision. They critically think the hell out of it. After all, isn't that what we pay professionals to do?

Let's say you take the car to a mechanic for the 'check engine' light, they will tell you what the check engine light is on for. If it seems odd, take it to a different mechanic and see what they say. 'Analyze the data', so you have a blown head gasket. Is this a certified mechanic or your sister's boyfriend? Is your mechanic unbiased? If you own a BMW and BMW says, 'we are the only ones that can fix that', is that true? Then you 'Establish Significance' - what pieces of information are most important? Now it is time to 'Make a decision' - identify possible conclusions, you could go to BMW or find a different mechanic. Lastly, you 'present or communicate' - maybe you speak to your spouse about your findings, the problem, the possible solutions and what you have decided to do.

Michael Tomaszewski laid this out perfectly. Critical thinking is a gift. If we did this more often as people, we would have less crime, less hatred, and less stress. Life's problems and work issues don't stop, but they do become less overwhelming when we think critically. As a leader, when I have a follower who can stop, assess, gather information, analyze it, and come to a suggestive conclusion, I am a happy man. I don't want to have to do all that for you. I want to be able to listen and agree or make a suggestion. This will allow me to move quickly onto the next thing on the agenda. It is frustrating to have a follower that demands a lot of attention and time to do their part. Not that coaching is not part of a leader's job, but when a leader tasks something, their hope is that they handle it. I once was told by a leader that his favorite word from one of his followers is 'Done!'. I fully understand why now. Now that follower can be trusted with more. This is how you establish trust and autonomy in your work. When you get shit done.

Another great example of critical thinking are attorneys. Let's say you are a defense attorney. You have an 18-year-old accused of murder. He swears on a stack of bibles he was nowhere near the crime scene. However, there are 3 witnesses who state they saw him there. The murder weapon has his fingerprints on it. You are racking your brain, trying to figure out how your client's fingerprints are on the murder weapon, when he indicates he was not at the scene. Later, you find out that he purchased that very murder weapon and returned it 3 days ago. It was a hammer, so he could hang a shelf in his garage. Then, you find out the hammer was restocked at the store and the suspect purchased that very hammer. The witnesses simply had mistaken identity, as the cell phone tower tracing indicates he was at home at the time of the murder. This is almost an identical situation I seen on TV of a young woman's trial. With duct tape, she was sent to prison and her kids taken away. For something, I truly believe she was innocent on. Without analyzing all the evidence, your client was surely going to jail. That is the impact of critical thinking. It can literally save someone's life. That is a characteristic of a follower. The same follower that before starting this book, had this big, ugly stigma of being someone who was weak and not confident. Who wasn't a leader? Blah, blah, blah.

Please if anything, let go of the stigma that being a follower is bad, it's not! It's necessary! Now maybe you are sitting there thinking; "Nelson, I work at a retail store, I hang clothes on racks." Ok! Great! That still requires you to think and think critically. Are you analyzing a planogram to lay out the garments in the store? Are you putting them back properly? That is critical thinking, and you should be proud of that! Don't let these lies society tells you, stick! Following is a proper way of becoming a great leader! Let's keep going.

The 'Yes' Men

One thing leaders often complain about in silence until it hits a boiling point is having to argue with their followers to get them to do something. Now, I am not referring to asking simple questions about what it is they are being asked to do. Followers aren't necessarily supposed to be acquiescent, rather compliant. In order for you to be a great follower, you must be compliant. Some might refer to this as being "coachable".

Being coachable or compliant is critical to the success of a follower. No one and I mean no one, wants a follower who won't listen. Why would anyone want to continually tell someone what to do and argue with them about doing it? Being compliant brings your leader a peace of mind. It also instills confidence in them about you. If you have children, you know exactly what I am talking about. When I ask one of my daughters to do something, that is all I want to do. Ask. I don't want to repeat or explain why it is fair for them to do it. I just want it done, by them. That may come across a little dictatorial, but I am the leader, and I am the one delegating. Remember, it is the leader's vision that you are helping to fulfill.

You aligned with this leader and their values, stick to your commitment, and help fulfill the greater purpose. Trust the leader you decided to follow. Now, let me be clear here. Compliance should never alter your values or beliefs. If something is wrong, it's wrong. Compliance doesn't mean doing something that is wrong. It means doing something within your beliefs and values that further the mission or vision you chose to get behind. It's changing your behavior, in essence, because someone has asked or persuaded you. Have you ever purchased something from a pushy salesperson? That is being compliant. If you were ever a teenager and caved into peer-pressure, you were compliant. Chances are that was something that differed from your values…but that's not what we are here to talk about. I have worked for leaders who asked for my compliance, and I did not agree with the action. So, in turn, I was non-compliant. And I am unapologetic about that. It was wrong and I didn't feel comfortable doing it.

      However, great leaders will never put you in a situation like that. Great leaders are trying to steer you into furthering the mission and/or vision. Trust them. Now, I want to go back to that "coachable" term many of us have heard over the years. That is a different form of compliance. Being coachable is being able to be told about yourself, whether that be your attitude, actions or behaviors that do not align with the overall mission and vision, or purpose. Sometimes you are coached on behaviors or patterns that were completely unintentional and innocent. Sometimes, your leader understands your action or behavior was deliberate. Regardless, they will and should always coach to it.

Let's say your leader comes to you Monday morning and asks you to run a report on the external internet usage. So, they want a report indicating what external websites each employee is visiting and how much time they have spent doing it. You agree to run the report, and you simply ask; "what intel are you looking to gather?" Your leader says, "Well our performance is down and as I walk through the office, I see a lot of staff on external sites for extended periods of time."

You run the report and you find that you are on that report as one of the highest external site visitors in the office. So, you change the parameters of the report when you run the data on you, so it looks like you visit the sites the least, you keep everyone else's data the same. You export it to an excel spreadsheet and hand it to your leader. Your leader then calls you in the office to discuss the report. What you didn't know is that your leader was really talking about what he sees you doing a lot of. He realizes the data doesn't add up, so he runs the report himself.

Now, your integrity and reliability are in question. He, as a good leader, must coach to this. He begins to talk to you about the importance of integrity and honesty. How utilizing company resources for personal entertainment is not a good use of company dollars. You begin to become defensive. You tell him that you work 8+ hours a day and aren't allowed to be on your personal cell phone. So, you use the computer to look at a few personal things of interest.

You aren't on any inappropriate sites or doing anything illegal, you don't see the big deal. Although, he just spent 20 minutes explaining the big deal. You are now being non-compliant. You failed to listen to his 'why' behind the 'what', and you are now telling your leader that it is no big deal that you waste a few hours a day on the internet for personal entertainment of some sort.

Not to mention, he can no longer trust you to run a simple report for him. So much trust has been lost in that little task, due to you being non-compliant. As a leader, it is going to take quite a bit of time to regain that trust with you. Being non-compliant has a damaging effect on your ability to be a great follower. Being a great follower is a foundational piece to being a great leader one day. Even if leadership isn't your overall goal, being trustworthy should be.

It wasn't me, it was the one-armed man

Forced responsibility is usually met with adverse reactions such as resistance. I wish I had the answer as to why people are so resistant to being held accountable to something they most likely agreed to, like their employment. Unfortunately, leaders are required to adapt to such persons and lead them in a way that brings them to a place of accountability. One thing I loathe as a leader is excuses. You give me a reason; I can deal with that, but an excuse just won't fly. I have worked in roles where my job was very numbers driven, daily. I had daily requirements that had to be met with particular numbers. When I wasn't performing where I should be, I tried to never make excuses. Just provide reasons.

We all know I am not where I need to be, whatever my excuse is, it won't be good enough to suffice the missing of the goal. So, why bother? Rather than coming up with excuses, I provided reasons. Reasons allow both the follower and the leader to brainstorm together on how to overcome whatever the obstacle is. For instance, let's say you work in sales. You have a daily sales quota of 8 "items" a day you must sell. It's 3:00 PM and you're at 4. Two hours before you are off the clock. Your leader asks; "what's up?" You respond with a reason that you are so busy with wrapping up yesterday's sales, that you didn't have time to make as many calls. An excuse might be "I just didn't have time". That would be inaccurate and false. You had 8 hours.

But you didn't manage those 8 hours well. Ok, if you say; "I didn't manage my time well", you are taking accountability and giving your leader something, they can work with. As a leader, I might say; "well where can I help?" or "Maybe we should consider knocking out today's sales the first half of your day and wrapping up yesterday's the second half". Of course, these are very generic and vague, but you get the idea. In order for you to be a great follower, you must be accountable.

Accountable followers can be utilized and trusted. If I can't utilize you as a leader, nor trust you to do what you promised, I don't need you. Is that harsh? Not really, it's the reality check of following a great leader. A great leader isn't going to let their team fail because one follower has decided to abandon their commitments on the team. Great leaders coach to a better performance, if you don't want to be better, we coach you out the organization. Another part of being accountable is creating checkpoints. When you are accountable, you consistently and frequently check-in to ensure you are on track.

For instance, your leader gives you a project to work on, a great follower starts by asking probing questions that may not have been answered when your leader gave you the project. From there, you are checking in with your leader to ensure you are on the right path. That tells your leader you are accountable to what they gave you and you want to ensure you complete this on time and correctly. Think about it from a place of marriage. Imagine one evening your spouse comes out the room, they are dressed nicely, ready to go out. They start heading to the door and say, "I'll see you later". You, not knowing where the heck they're going, ask; "where are you going?" They respond with; "out". Every bad and insecure thought begins to surface, due to their lack of accountability to the marriage. You trust has drastically dipped because they didn't want to have the conversation about their evening plans. They didn't discuss it with you in advance. They didn't even invite you.

Of course, you have a problem on your hands. The same is true with a great leader who has an unaccountable follower. The leader has a problem on their hands. There's a saying I use for people who have endless amounts of excuses; "You have a problem for every solution". These types of people don't want help. They don't want to get better. They want to bathe in their excuses and soak in the "woe is me" mentality. Until you hold yourself accountable to your failures, setbacks, and anything in your life you don't like, you will never move forward. Until you own your lack of performance, bury the excuses, and accept accountability, you'll never be a great follower. Remember, not everyone wants to be a leader, that defaults you to a follower, you might as well be the best follower you can be.

Now, I want to be crystal clear on the difference between accountable and responsible.

Responsible means to be answerable for something within your scope. Leaders are responsible for their staff's performance. Accountable is to give account or report something. There is no responsibility to the overall performance of the team. Even if the team missing their goal because of your performance, it still falls responsible to the leader. You are responsible for your individual performance, but not the team. I always laugh watching sports fans blame the one player who made a last second error, like a missed field goal. The field goal kicker misses the kick, and they blame that sole player for the loss.

Technically, it's the team that let it be that close where it came down to a field goal, therefore, multiple people are accountable to this performance. The coach is responsible for the loss. Accountability, once understood and accepted, makes life so much easier and being a follower so much more rewarding. Another critical piece on being accountable is owning your emotions. Emotions can run hot when a leader is holding a follower accountable. You and your leader or employer agreed that you would perform at a certain level to be a contributing member of the team, when you did not do that, it was not your leader's fault. Now, your leader now has an obligation to have a difficult conversation with you. I can assure you, no leader wants to have these conversations, but as a great leader, we must.

Emotions can derail productivity and a relationship with your leader. Harness those emotions and redistribute them in your performance. Allow your emotions to be a driving force behind performing at an optimal level. That is ok. Just don't harness your emotions to hold a grudge towards your leader or organization. Being accountable also inspires confidence in yourself. You can take complete responsibility for knocking it out the park. You can be proud of yourself and all you've been able to accomplish. I guarantee you unaccountable people don't get this luxury. A.A.R., you get to do this when you're accountable.

You get to accept, acknowledge, and release. **A**ccept where you are, **A**cknowledge what needs to be done and **R**elease any doubt that you are unable to achieve it. It's powerful when you are that clear in your mind. You simply empower yourself to accomplish the goal. One reason unaccountable people love to throw out when they are being unaccountable is determinism, essentially cause and effect. Because of this, I did this. Because emails wouldn't stop, I couldn't get this done. Or because this system isn't working well, I wasn't able to hit my goal. It's really easy to fall into this mindset, and it is a really slippery slope.

The last thing you want is for your leader to expect an excuse from you when they talk to you. You want them to believe you are going to be accountable. So, how do you make yourself accountable? The first thing you must do is understand the expectations. If you don't understand the goal or expectations, there's no way to hold yourself accountable to it. The second thing is to let go of any pride you may have. It's not about your ego, it's about your commitment. The third thing is own it. If you missed the mark, you missed it. It wasn't your computer program, it wasn't the limited hours in the day, it was the fact you missed it.

The fourth thing is to manage your time wisely, know what hurdles you have in your day and manage your time around those. If you have several meetings, make sure they end for you on time. If you must excuse yourself from the meeting to keep track, do so. Fifth, and an important one, do not over commit yourself. You know if you can do it or not. Don't over commit to make yourself look good, because at the end, you won't. Sixth, plan for success. Make a detailed plan that is going to help you become successful and accountable. Also, plan for variations of change. Routine is not king. We love routine, but business and life are anything but routine. Keep your head on a swivel and be agile! Lastly, look back at what you've done and what you were able to accomplish. Celebrate the small wins and be proud of yourself! You are going to be your biggest cheerleader, and you should be. If the goal was to go to the gym 5 days this week and you did it, be proud! Who cares if you didn't lift as much weight as you wanted to, you went to the gym!

All in all, accountability is your friend in success. I have never seen a successful leader, someone promoted, a healthy relationship or someone who is highly respected that is unaccountable. Accountability is an attractive trait. It attracts success, a great reputation and overall happiness. When you hold yourself accountable you tend to make better decisions, because you know you are going to have to answer for the one's you make. Every action has a reaction. A decision is an action. Be sure to make the right one by holding yourself accountable.

Thank you to all, and to all a goodnight

One thing I wanted to teach my kids at an early age was to be grateful for all they had. For them to understand that not everyone gets to be in their shoes. Also, that some people are praying for what they get the luxury of having. In order for you to be a great follower, you must express gratitude. Notice I said "express" gratitude. That is an intentional action. You are showing someone you are grateful. How do we know people are excited or happy? They express it on their faces. Expression is confirmation. Gratitude is a magnet for more. When you don't feel entitled, you are grateful.

When you don't see your blessings as normal, you become grateful. When you do, you become unsettled. As a society in general, we need to learn to become more settled. More grateful. More content. When I say "content", I do not mean lack of ambition. I mean being comfortable with what we have and appreciating it. My friend Brandon Perritte once said; "What you fail to honor, you lose". Boy, was he ever spot on! Gratitude aligns with honor. Gratitude shows thankfulness for what you have. There is so much to be thankful for. Life, health, a job, your leader, your income, your family, your birthplace, your car. We can list endless things to be grateful for.

Gratitude isn't always inward. As a matter of fact, grateful people are usually selfless people. They are so grateful; they want to help others get there. A great follower is grateful and wants to help their leader be successful, because they are grateful for them. One glaring issue in our society is entitlement. The world we get to live in, does not revolve around us. As a matter of fact, start using that phrase "get to" and replace "have to" with it. Let me give you an example; "I can't go out tonight because I *HAVE TO* go to work". Now let's read it differently; "I can't go out tonight because I *GET TO* go to work".

Doesn't that sound much healthier? There are thousands, if not millions, looking for jobs. You are fortunate enough to have one, be grateful! Perspective is critical to changing your viewpoint. Changing your perspective from entitled to grateful, will help you change your viewpoint. I was at a local *Starbucks* one time, I watched someone order their very specific drink, they told the Barista; "I want 125 degrees, if it's 120, I'll know". It took everything in me not to defend the Barista and tell this jerk to grow up. However, that wasn't my responsibility. The Barista kindly acknowledged their demand and their passive aggressive threat and made their drink. But this level of entitlement is gross.

One aspect of being grateful is saying; "Thank you". It is remarkable how many people don't say 'thank you'. A simple 'thank you', almost seems like a daunting task for civilization. We don't use gratefulness as a tool for manipulation. We don't say 'thank you' for a 'you're welcome'. Is it common courtesy to say; 'you're welcome'? Yes. But did you say, 'thank you' for a 'you're welcome'? No. If you did, you aren't thankful or grateful. You're well-mannered. Entitlement can be a personality disorder as well. I am not a professional psychologist, by any means, but many scholarly journals and blogs discuss entitlement as a personality disorder.

You find it a lot in narcissists. One way they discuss how to change this mentality is to celebrate others. I absolutely love this. Celebrating others and genuinely being happy for them, brings us so much joy internally. It is ok for someone to get something you really want before you do. Maybe someone gets married before you. Or someone gets promoted before you. That is completely fine! It doesn't mean it's not going to happen to you. Celebrate them! This is a book about being a great follower, but you will not get there without changing behaviors.

One fun practice I like is a Gratitude Wall, whether in your home or in the workplace. Where you take a simple yellow sticky note and write something you are grateful for, you put it on the wall. That simple example encourages others to do the same. Soon enough, you have a culture of gratitude and a team that is appreciating life itself a little more. Many organizations have internal recognition methods that allow you to acknowledge your colleagues in the office. I highly recommend utilizing that tool to do so. It will begin to help you learn more about gratitude and how to express it. It will most likely help you gain some friends in the organization as well. Your network is important. The point of this is not to gain a network, but to genuinely express gratitude in your everyday life. I want to see the people who want to be followers, be successful at it. Great followers are grateful and express gratitude. Your leader trusts you to lead a big project? Be grateful. Your leader asks you to do something that may be inconvenient in the moment? Be grateful.

Sometimes we can feel under-valued and under-appreciated in the workplace, that can lead to an attitude of ungratefulness. They aren't delegating because they are lazy, they are doing it because they trust you can get it done the best. There are much more brutally honest ways to bring someone off their high-horse and back down to this planet where they shouldn't be entitled and should be grateful, but those aren't healthy or mature. As individual humans, we need to monitor ourselves when we get those feelings and really assess if it's just a negative thought, or do you honestly feel that your leader under-values you and does not appreciate you? Do you have concrete examples that are nearly impossible to misinterpret? If so, be open and transparent with your leader. Let them know, respectfully, how you are feeling and why. A great leader will be humble and allow themselves to acknowledge their own behaviors and apologize. After all, you're following them because they're great and have aligned values with you. This shouldn't be a moment of fear or uncertainty. Gratefulness is a magnet for more. Remember that. I want to share a story about a gentleman named

"Marcus". I don't want to recap, so I am going to directly quote The Lifeblog by Gratitude (2022) here. They released the amazing story of gratitude from Marcus and here it is "I'm Marcus. I'm a very grateful person these days. It wasn't always like that. My story is basically, I've had a terrifying drug addiction for most of my life. And during most of that, I was pretty ungrateful for many things that I should have been grateful for.

But my vision and my perception, everything was so clouded. So yeah, I was very negative, I was very depressed, even almost even suicidal at certain points of it. And I wasn't a happy person at all. It was dark. And towards the end, it became extremely dark, it really wasn't a nice place, wasn't a nice feeling. And today, I'm talking about gratitude and the impact that's had on my life. And one of the first things I did when I surrendered to the fact that my life could not go on this way, I couldn't kid myself anymore.

I joined this fellowship and one of the things that were suggested to do, especially for newcomers, like me, was to write a gratitude list of 10 things that you were grateful for every morning, or every evening, or any point.

And when I started doing this, I was told not to just suddenly stop the things the substances I was taking. Because when I tried to do that a couple of times, I had quite severe fits and seizures, and I was told that these are very dangerous, and I might not actually come out of them.

So, I was told to try to gradually medicate myself. I wasn't in a position to put myself into a proper medical facility, I didn't have the money. And I was at a very critical point. So, when I first started my gratitude, I was still in the midst of all that madness.

And my gratitude list was pretty sparse. It was like a little withered tree. By the grace of God, I still had a roof over my head, and I still had food to eat. So those were the things I was massively grateful for. I was grateful for the air I was breathing. I continued with it.

It was something that I never, ever forgot to do. And I didn't sleep properly at that time, either. Quite often, my plan was to do it in the morning, it was on a WhatsApp group, I would have normally submitted my list at about four o'clock in the morning. I just had nothing to do and I'll just be thinking that's the one thing that I've got to do because you can't start doing the other work until you've actually got clean. In my work with the fellowship I was doing, the main thing was your gratitude lists and reaching out to other people.

I continued with it my list, and I started being able to notice more and more stuff to be grateful for. The attitude of gratitude started developing. And it did take some practice.

The first little while, it seemed a bit like it wasn't going anywhere. But given how long I've been ungrateful for, to how quickly this attitude of gratitude was able to develop is just incredible.

And the changes I've experienced in my mind, I'm grateful. I just have to take one step, and there's just a whole myriad of new things to be grateful for. And I love life. And if you'd said this to me, six months ago, that this is how you're going to feel and this is what every day is going to be like, I would have laughed.

I continued with my gratitude lists, they developed, and they grew. At some point, a few months in, I finally managed to get completely clean. I did that all by myself without any medical assistance.

Very suddenly, just overnight, I decided one more time to just go for it, even though it was against the advice of the medical people. And this time, I didn't have the seizures and the fits. That was a massive thing on my list.

I said it was 24 hours and all the other people in the group said, "Yeah! Wonderful!" For me, that was a massive thing, just to get through 24 hours. It's hundreds of days now but that first day, I was so grateful for that.

And I was speaking to other people in the fellowship, and someone introduced me to the Gratitude app. And, I thought, "Yeah, that seems pretty cool. I've got photographs on there; I will read up the daily sentence." I make one or two entries every single day to the app, and I love having that.

That's the first thing I do in the morning is I get up and I go to my knees, and I pray. And then, the next thing I do is write my gratitude list. And then to put on this WhatsApp group, there are lots of other people that appreciate seeing it.

Because a lot of the people in the group don't actually like to submit something themselves, they just like to read other people's stuff. So, I always do that. And I love how the app prompts me all throughout the day, it'll just have little questions and little prompts, and it just sets off these little neuron neurological paths.

"Oh, yeah, actually, though, but I do have that to be grateful. And that worked out quite nicely." I've had a complete transformation of my mind. So, the first thing I'm grateful for is God. I do think that the next thing is the attitude of gratitude.

Because that's the thing that flipped my mind from complete negativity. I'm talking about it. And so, I've just got a massive smile on my face. And I feel like I could carry on for the next two hours.

I'm grateful every single day. And I realize, my life was always like this. I always had this amount of stuff to be grateful for. But I missed it, I had this other set of glasses on, and I couldn't see any of it.

There are things I could complain about, I guess. But that's all I used to focus on in the past. And now, I focus on the positive things. And I will say, every step I take, as soon as I open the door, as soon as I come back home, there is just so much stuff to be grateful for, it's wonderful.

And I love my life now. I love God. I love my life. I love everyone. I used to, it sounds painful to say, but I used to hate everyone. I used to hate myself. I used to hate everybody else. I was an angry person.

That's how it was. And now it's completely different. I've got lots of dear friends I've met in recent times. My old friendships have come back because a lot of people were very worried about me, people that really did love me, but they couldn't be around me.

My close family stayed close-ish but from an arm's distance. Now, I'm quite a popular person. My days are full. I have to go to work, obviously. As soon as I'm finished working phone calls, I've got people coming around, people who want me to go out.

And these are just all things I can be grateful for. So now it's like whenever the app pops up with a little question, I'll take it quite seriously. I feel like sometimes when I'll just scroll through the list, I'm like, "Wow!"

There are pictures and this and that. And it's just full of love and smiles and gratitude. And I just think, wow, this is amazing. I'm not exaggerating when I say it has been absolutely key, and it is one of the first things that's taken me from a really terrifying place. Now I'm in a sunny Meadow with those rainbows. And may this continue". Marcus gets it! Powerful.

1+1 is definitely 11

I have led many teams that in employee engagement surveys have stated that they think people have been promoted that didn't deserve it. Do you see how awful of a mindset that is when you read it? First and foremost, there's a process to getting promoted, you can't just give someone a job. Secondly, you have no idea what that person may have had to do to get that role. They could've been our friend Marcus who had the incredible story of gratitude. So, how could you possibly know if they deserved it? In order for you to be a great follower, you must be competent.

When I say incompetent, people think you are insulting them. You really aren't. If someone is incompetent, they are someone who does not have sufficient training and experience or knowledge and other qualities; that allow them to assist you properly. The level of competence required will depend on the complexity of the situation and the help you need. It's not that they're stupid, or remedial, or uneducated. It is merely, they do not have the skillset to do the job you would need them to do. In the example of the employee engagement survey, the person complaining that someone else got promoted, before them, undeservingly, I would consider that type of individual incompetent to even do the job the person I promoted was able to do. Your attitude is missing so much.

I can exemplify attitude; I can't teach it. You choose your attitude every day, like you chose those shoes you're wearing. If you don't like the result of it, *CHANGE YOUR DAMN SHOES*! Competence is such an important characteristic in a great follower. Competence generates trust. Let me put it this way. You are having heart surgery, you are on the table in front of someone who may have been deserving of that promotion to chief surgeon, but their boss thought they weren't competent enough…in front of you, ready to slice you open…. you completely trust them?

Of course, you'd never know that about your medical provider, but this is how your leader builds trust with you. They can see your competence and can trust you with more. When that person that did get the job does well, the rest of the team will also trust their leader's decision-making even more so. Competence is so important. One way to help become more competent, is to speak less. I remember when I was young, people used to tell me; "God gave you one mouth and two ears for a reason". To shut up and listen more. I have actually never learned anything from me speaking. Nothing. Not a damn thing. Isn't that funny?

Talking less allows for you to learn and grow. Eat the meat and leave the bones, of course. Meaning keep what applies to you or aligns to your personal values. And ignore what doesn't. When people know you are a good listener, they want to tell you stuff.

Great stuff! Sometimes you get people who are really not telling you great stuff. Stuff that won't move you forward or give you a healthy mindset, that is what you need to ignore. We are adults, we know the type of speech I am referring to, there's no need to be told. Unless you aren't competent? See what I did there? I just couldn't resist. The stages of learning model are a fantastic way to try and understand competence. It's such a great illustration

There are 4 stages of competence. The first stage is *Unconscious Incompetence*. When my two daughters were 3 years old, they didn't know they couldn't write in cursive, and probably didn't care. That is the unconscious incompetence stage. The next stage is the *Conscious Incompetence* stage. If my daughters still couldn't write in cursive at 6, but knew what cursive was and I asked them to; "Write me a sentence in cursive", they would know they can't. They would be aware or conscious of their incompetence. The third stage is the *Conscious Competence* stage.

My daughters are now 18 and fully aware and exposed to cursive. They practice their cursive periodically, they are paying attention to their pen stroke game and intentionally, smoothly guiding their hands as they write me a sentence. Moving from stage to stage can be challenging and difficult. You are growing and being stretched. It can be painful, and mistakes will be made, but it's necessary to keep moving. That is certainly true from stage two to three.

They wrote many ugly cursive sentences before they were able to get to the *John Hancock* level cursive. The fourth stage, my daughters will be writing full letters in cursive, they may even use cursive more than print or block script. They'll make very few mistakes; it will be like second nature to them. That is called *Unconscious Competence*. This is where they don't realize how skilled they are in cursive writing. It's the "this old thing?!" mentality. Someone compliments their cursive, they respond with; "This old thing?! I've been writing like this since 'Nam girl!"

Some believe there is a fifth stage, that where the student becomes the teacher. It would be like my daughters now teach a penmanship course. From not being able to do it at 6, to teaching a course! That's a lot of growth! Competence is bigger than knowing more than someone else, it's about growth and growth potential, attitude, discipline, outward thinking. It's a melting pot of positive attributes. "I closed more sales than Mark! I should be the Sales Manager!" Sound familiar? Like Elsa…." *Let it go!, Let it goooooo*!" It is such a toxic mindset and vibe to let off. It's not 'woe is me'…competence is 'next time it will be me'. Do you see the power of having competence, as a great follower? This is what your leader is looking for! Competence!

Once you truly feel you are at a level of competence that can be given more, as a follower, raise the expectation bar. For instance, maybe you are given a presentation to do. Your boss has never challenged you with anything like this, so they're expectation level isn't incredibly high. This is your opportunity to flip the lens of your leader and show them your level of confidence. This is your chance to be at the helm of the boat in extremely choppy waters and show the captain (who gave you your chance at the helm, to show you could be a future captain) you can get the ship through this!

  I sincerely apologize to anyone who works in the waters with this (what I am sure is) an incredibly inaccurate depiction of the promotion process in the open seas. I am ignorant to the, what I believe, is a much more daunting promotion process. When trying to convey competence, pay attention to your body language. It says much more than you think. Make eye contact and smile. In meetings, sit closer to the front. Participate with great question asking. Too many people's confidence equates to competence.

  Another way to increase competence awareness and buy-in is to be positive! No one believes your competent when you're negative. You can't even control your negativity; how could you be competent? Don't sell yourself short or put off a vibe that isn't really you, by being negative. You owe yourself more than that. You have a purpose on this earth, maybe that purpose is to be such a great follower, you help a leader achieve a bigger purpose other than something for yourself. Being a great leader is nothing, to not be excited about. Very poor

English, I know. It just felt right writing it. You are an anchor to much bigger purpose. You can feel very confident in that. No one follows a leader to help them achieve a personal goal for personal gain. NO! We are attracted to much more than that. We are attracted to much bigger visions.

Becoming more competent is also found in habits. Intentionally investing in your craft is a great example. Maybe you have an online learning system integrated in your workplace. Maybe you can job shadow with the role you want to move into. Maybe you can talk about your development with your leader in your next 1:1, they can reach out to the leadership of that team and advise them they have an employee interested in moving down that career path. From there, you can gain a ton of competence. Most importantly, you can clearly see where to not waste your time! You will find that you want to avoid negativity, unhealthy thinking and speech, ungratefulness, and dishonor. They are your biggest growth killers in life. Your mind and your speech are life changing. They can change your life for the good or the bad.

You think it, it becomes words and manifests to reality. Only if it were that easy to the positive side. Going positive requires work! You have to avoid certain people, certain music and certain tv. Then you must intentionally replace negative thoughts, with positive ones. *YOU HAVE TO PUT THAT WORK IN, SON!* But the reward? Oh baby, you can't even fathom how good life gets. It is real! You haven't kept reading this book because you are uninterested in becoming a great follower. You are interested. You might as well apply what I am telling you.

Unless you are uninterested in a rewarding life, operating in the purpose that is on you, which leads to a passion, which leads to fulfillment. If what I am saying isn't your thing and you want to chase some else's purpose and feeling like you are making no progress in life and in a hamster wheel, stop reading. *IT IS TIME TO BE GREAT AND IGNORE THE RHETORIC AROUND BEING A FOLLOWER, IT'S A GREAT POSITION TO BE IN!* Do you think Tom Brady, the offensive leader of the Patriots and Buccaneers for several years, regrets following Bill Belichick or Bruce Arians? Nope! He has 7 super bowl rings from it. Both Belichick and Arians needed their follower, Tom Brady. And Tom Brady needed his leaders, Arians, and Belichick. Michael Jordan needed Phil Jackson, and vice versa. Shaq and Kobe needed Phil Jackson.

Which just proves my point of following the right person can get you a lot of exposure, accolades and fulfillment. But they didn't do it for that. They did it because they understood their purpose! They weren't called to coach (leader), they were called to play (follower) and the world loved them because of it. Do you think Bill Belichick is sitting there saying; "I did the coaching, why does he get so much shine?"

No! He is so happy to see his follower's success, it gives him a sense of fulfillment in knowing he was a part of it. When I started this characteristic, I started with competence, and I am still there. This is all about the power of competence. Help your leader and be competent.

Bonnie and Clyde

This characteristic is a sensitive one. I can already hear the argument back on this one. "What about them? They will let you go with no notice for a buck!" If you haven't caught it, I am talking about being committed. In order for you to be a great follower, you must be committed. Being committed does not mean not getting hurt from time to time. If you are going to accept the vulnerability of the leader trusting you to help them achieve a goal, then you have to stay committed. When organizations do things like layoffs, it isn't personal. They aren't targeting you, it's just a numbers game. I have been laid off personally, so I understand the feeling. I was laid off from a company I wanted to stay at, and one that I saw myself staying for a while at. Didn't matter, I was let go because I was the newest member of the team. Nothing personal.

    I was laid off by something I voted for by the way. That's a whole other story. But I was committed. After being laid off, I went back to the organization when they offered me another position. I wanted to work there. Unfortunately, it didn't work out. But I wasn't looking for other employment when I was there. I like the team I worked with. I enjoyed the leader I worked for. I enjoyed the work I did. I was good. At the time, prior to being laid off, I was not thinking about promotion. So, I never had a development conversation with this boss. I would imagine they would've been helpful. All in all, I say that to say I was committed and got laid off by the very organization I was committed to. Some qualities I have noticed in committed people is passion, holistic team vision and happiness. They are incredibly passionate about what they do and the vision behind it. They defend it like it's their child. They are advocates for what they do. They proudly state how long they've been at their employer and often quote their leaders. They are innovative, finding unique ways to streamline work processes. When they vision for the team, they vision everyone winning together and the team or organization, being successful. It's almost majestic! Like a unicorn, riding a rainbow, with The *Ultimate Warrior* holding a machine gun on the back of the unicorn riding the rainbow! Like real majestic. I'm joking but, seriously, it's amazing.

Commitment is not just at the organization level, it's also at the departmental level. For instance, you have a meeting with your boss. They are going to roll-out a new policy or procedure you don't love. It isn't against any personal values, just not going to be the most fun season when they roll this out. Instead of going back to the team and complaining about it and making it harder to create buy-in for your leader, you said nothing. You express your concern to your boss, but it stays within that office. No one ever knows you disagreed with your boss. When rolled out, you show support for the decision. That is committed. Some may read that and think "I'm being fake, I can't do that". You are not being fake; you are being committed to the greater purpose or the leader themselves. Commitment is a stretch assignment for many, but it is the only way you can be considered a great follower. Commitment is similar to being accountable. Within accountability is commitment. Committed to getting the work done that you are accountable to.

For a short season in my life, I worked at *Nordstrom*. An excellent company, with excellent values and a commitment to what their family started. When I started at *Nordstrom*, they shared a story of a store employee who showed a next-level demonstration of commitment. A store employee received a call from a frantic woman. She explains over the phone that she was in their store yesterday. She said she lost her engagement ring there. This employee was very familiar with morning routine and knew that the bags from the vacuums hadn't been emptied yet. He thought; "Maybe her ring is in there". What did this guy do? He dug through all the freaking vacuum bags and found this ladies engagement ring and returned it to her.

That is commitment to an organization! I was so proud to be a Nordstrom employee when I heard that story. I shared that story so many times, it is unbelievable. It is such a cool story and a great example of a committed follower. Committed employees do whatever it takes to move the needle, even if it means taking on extra work, or staying beyond their schedule. "That is not within my job description" is the new "It's not my job". Almost makes me want to vomit. Such a poor attitude and one that adds no value to the team. A great follower wants to help. As leaders, it is our jobs to not burn that person out or take advantage of their capacity. It is important you understand those boundaries as well, as a great follower. Know where to stop. That doesn't mean before you even try to take on more. "Oh, you're not going to over work me!" Relax, they just asked for you to take on a little more. Be a hot follower! What is the point of being a luke-warm follower? Be on fire for your purpose!

Committed followers get great benefits from being committed: consistent work history and a healthy work-ethic. Let's start backwards on this one. It is incredibly healthy to not run away from a tough job or chase the dollar. You learn to fight. You learn to adjust and grow; you build healthy habits. You work hard – and that's a great thing. Just because you were committed. Then because of your commitment, you don't look like a job hopper on your resume. Having to explain why you have had 6 jobs in 5 years at 6 different organizations. It's ok to stay put. Don't compare your unedited scenes, to the final cut. It's ok if your friend from high school is making $30k more a year than you. That's fine, you'll get there through hard work and intentional actions that help you move in that direction. If you are following a leader that is a great leader, they will intentionally develop you, if you talk about your career path with them. I am from a generation that hops jobs like puddles when you were a kid. It is such a bad trait. Given in the rapid world we live in, it makes complete sense. The all-knowing, all-amazing Google search is a great example. We can

Google anything and get a response back in less than seconds. We live in a world where someone can perform a basic action on video, 3 million people will watch it and share it with their closest circle and that content creator makes $100k. Everything is right now. How can I get to better, fast? Unfortunately, we weren't ready for this phenomenon. We applied it to everything in life. Including our careers. I need to be at this position, by this date. Rather than soaking a little. Soaking up as much as we possibly could about what it is we do, now. Becoming the best at what we do, now. Do I believe that it was Google's intentions to make us impatient, uncommitted for an extended length of time humans, of course not. I believe they wanted to supply the world access to information at a faster rate, and that is something I am forever grateful for. We have to get better at soaking. Marinate a little where you are. The final product is much better.

Kendrick Lamar

There's a song that gets me so excited from the energy it produces. The artist is Compton, California born rapper, Kendrick Lamar. He has a song titled; "Humble". In the Chorus he says, "Sit down. Be Humble". The instruction in that is powerful. Sit down, be humble. In order for you to be a great follower, you must be humble. Humility is another descriptive word that receives a bad reputation, just like follower. How is a person with humility, generally described as? You might hear someone call them insecure, or submissive. Humility is a super-power! Just ask Kendrick!

Seriously, it is. I can't tell you how many arrogant salespeople I have worked with. Good Lord! Were they good salespeople? Yes. But rather than understanding that their gift, doesn't make them more valuable to society than the next person. They spoke in 3rd person and were incredibly condescending. They acted as though; it was such an honor to speak to them. It leaked out of their pores. They could've had monumentally successful careers, but no one wanted to be around them. So, in turn, their path was missed (in my humble opinion). The gift is still there. They didn't realize they were followers. I won't say the name of the financial institutions I am referring to, but they were the leaders, not the sales reps. They changed our sales quotas without notice or approval, they reduced payouts for certain items sold, they were the ones in charge. Yet, these individuals walked around as though they were. They didn't work as a team, they sandbagged sales, it was a very self-absorbed style of working.

Being a great follower is the opposite, it requires humility. Great followers know how to sustain relationships. They know how to win people over with common courtesy and a magnetic spirit of humility. Their listening skills are incredible, drawing more curiosity, adding value to conversations, getting more answers, and building their influence. Humility opens doors. Let's say you're on a date, the person goes on for 45 minutes talking about themselves. You finally get your chance, and you talk for maybe 10 mins because your date didn't ask any questions, are you annoyed? Of course! How arrogant to go on and on about yourself and seem disinterested when you start talking. Humility is an important, crucial piece to being a great follower.

I worked for an organization where I was brought in from the outside, to lead a team. I was by no means a subject matter expert for who I was leading. I struggled with a particular direct report. To a point I thought I offended this individual, that's how thick the tension would get. Well come to find out, this person applied for the job I got, now I was leading them. That is fine, if the follower has humility. However, this person was mad about it. So, when I couldn't answer a question without additional research, she would make an innuendo that I was slightly under-qualified for my role. Not in such a direct manner, but it was obvious. When you lack humility, you build barriers and poison relationships you may not want to build or poison. If you are never wrong, better than your leader (to you), or your idea is the best on the team ALWAYS, you lack humility. If you are too big to follow, you are too small to lead. Humility is one of the most obvious negative traits of a bad follower.

  One area that still seems to be an issue in the marketplace is being coachable. As many times that poor followers have heard this said to them, you would think it would've spread by now in the bad follower community. But no luck. It is still an issue. It isn't an issue of coachability, it's an issue of humility. The marketplace needs more humble followers. Can we get some more Kendrick Lamar's? If you are too proud to hear correction, you are going to walk yourself into the hole you're digging. The iconic Lauryn Hill said, "If I am the messenger and you block me, you block the message". Don't block your message! Sit down, be humble!

Yoga

Imagine if you could wake up every day, go to work, come home and everything went smooth – no changes, or adjustments to what you like? What would that be like? Perfection? Well truth of the matter is life is not like that. Life has obstacles. Life requires agility. Life requires reasoning and understanding. In order for you to be a great follower, you must be flexible. Flexibility is going to help you sustain happiness. Flexibility is achieved by reasoning.

When I say reasoning, I mean being reasonable. Life has constant change. Because of that, businesses have constant change. As an employee of a company and a follower of a leader, you must understand this. Things change. It's not personal. It's not ridiculous. It's inconvenient at times, but you'll live. I promise. So far, you have survived 100% of the days that were hard and required you to be flexible. Relax. All will be well. This too shall pass. Followers that exhibit excellent flexibility bring peace to a leader. It also brings peace to a team. Because, if you are an F.W.I. and you aren't flexible, your anxious and irritable because of it, you are toxic for a culture. Your poor leader has to try and clean up the oil spill of a culture mess you made.

Your employer will have change that is inconvenient, and you don't agree with. If it doesn't counter your values and principles, roll with it. Show the team you are behind it and may not totally understand it, but you're optimistic. It's ok to not agree, but it's not ok to vocalize that across your team. It's hard enough for the leader to deliver the news that may not be accepted well, it's extremely hard to go behind you and clean up your poo mouth.

 Let me give you a great example. COVID-19. You see that and you are feeling some type of way. I guarantee that. When COVID-19 turned into a pandemic, it flipped the world upside down. COVID-19 had more of an impact in the world than Apple. COVID-19 changed how we travel, it changed how we dine, it changed how far we stand from each other, everyone wore a surgical mask and created other masks. The internet became even more important to businesses and new millionaires were born. Employers were stuck with a really hard choice: send everyone home to work from there or keep them in the office. Work-from-home was a massively common term. So was "you're on mute". Every single business was forced to make that decision, or the state made it for you for some. Your employer had so many questions to answer before making that decision: Are we equipped to send people home? Will our culture die? Do we have the leaders to lead a team remotely? Do we have the systems to work from home? Will we still be profitable? Countless questions!

Yet when employers took "too long" to make the decisions, followers got disgruntled. Complaining that other organizations have already sent their staff home. Or they really want us to catch this. On top of that, they were faced with another massive decision: mandate vaccinations or not? Oh my was that a shit show. The American pride rose to the surface and complained about "their rights" and how this political party is for the vaccine and the other one isn't. The conspiracy theory that they were planting computer chips in us that were small enough to be inside the LIQUID vaccine and still operate and fit through the needle. Then once through the needle and floating randomly through your veins, it was tracking us. If you are reading this 10 or more years after COVID-19, you are probably thinking America had lost their minds, the answer is an emphatic YES!!!! If I am lucky enough to have this book cycle through our library system in 2040, I want to say I am sorry. We failed you in 2020, we had a huge opportunity to change the future and we missed it.

Anyways, I say all of that just to say when your employer finally made their decisions, they had people on both sides of the fence. Employees who disagreed with the decision, complained so much. This change they didn't want made them angry so bad, they were on national TV complaining. Flexibility was the name of the game in 2020. If you meet any adult who was a leader in 2020, ask them about building a culture or flexibility, they most likely mastered it. COVID was hard. It was incredibly challenging to lead and be successful.

Leadership can sometimes be lonely as is but having absolutely no one around you but your cat or dog and wondering if other leaders are facing the same challenges, you were crazy lonely. *Zoom* saved many organizations. I hope for the opportunity to speak to *Zoom* staff and thank them for such amazing work. For saving leaders and followers from depression and joblessness. For connecting organizations, virtually, with each other. *Zoom* you are heroes in American history!

Flexibility is a cornerstone for a great follower. It's the cornerstone of a successful leader. One way a leader can tell if they have a great follower with flexibility, is their calmness in adversity. Great followers with flexibility are able to remain calm in adversity, due to their strong ability to quickly pivot. This is only adverse or difficult because it's unknown. In those very moments is where the great followers emerge. They stand in the face of the unknown and position themselves to pivot where necessary. Not whine, complain, and talk about how you like the "old way". The old way is gone and here we are, what are you going to do?

How can a leader rely on you when you are only one way? They can't ask you to do anything that you don't normally do. Just re-read that. The problem in that is crystal clear. Keep your head on a swivel. Be alert and ready to be flexible, you'll add a significant amount of value to your team and your leader. Plus, you'll be easier to be around in your personal life as well. No one likes to hang around a tight ass. So, the plan was to go to the club, but they switched it to the bar instead, ok? Go to the bar, I am sure they have music and alcohol. See! Just like that, you are that guy/gal everyone wants to call to come hang out!

Old Faithful

There's an old saying when something is trustworthy, people call it "old faithful". I can trust this particular thing is going to do what it was designed to do every time. For some people, it's their old pickup truck. For some people, it's the hot comb their mother had when she was a kid, that you are now using as an adult. Maybe for you it's a skillet. For a leader, it's a great follower. In order for you to be great follower, you must be trustworthy. There's a classic sports photo of Dwayne Wade and LeBron James when they played together in Miami. Dwayne Wade is throwing a no-look alley-oop behind him in the air to LeBron James. What makes the photo absolutely fantastic is that Lebron James is throwing down the dunk, and Dwayne Wade has his arm's out absolutely knowing LeBron James is dunking the ball and he did not miss the pass.

The only way Dwayne Wade could be so confident is because he knows LeBron James is trustworthy to do what he was created to do in that moment. LeBron James is "old faithful" to Dwayne Wade. Great leaders are looking for those very similar great followers. They're ready to toss you an alley-oop but you have to be old faithful and catch it and dunk it! You can't just catch it and land back on the ground. You ruined it if you do.

Chances are if you are reading this, you are not a 6'8 250 lbs. N.B.A. legend, so that will never be a situation you are in. So, what does look like for you in real life? You follow through with what you say you're going to do. If you can do that, you will build that type of reputation. Another great indicator is that you can be trusted with personal information. You are not a gossip or sharing other people's secrets. Trustworthy people understand that when someone is vulnerable with you, they are expecting a high-level of respect with their information. Don't share it.

Being around a great leader can sometimes give you access. They do not owe you access, it's just a perk of affiliation. With said access, you must be trustworthy. Why? Because you will hear things that is not to be shared. Not because it's morally inappropriate, but because it's sensitive to the culture. Maybe it's too early to release that information? Maybe you heard of an upcoming change that you know is going to affect the team? Either way, being trustworthy is foundational here. Your leader is looking for that level of maturity and understanding. It is your job to understand that. Remember, what's understood doesn't need to be explained.

You know, I am an unorthodox leader. I am a little blunt and charismatic at times. I say things that maybe some leaders wouldn't say, but I am who I am. Meaning, I am me, 2-4-7, 3-6-5. That helped me become trustworthy with leaders. I was authentic. Whether you think I am too much, or crass at times, I'm authentic. I am not hiding who I am. I grew up poor in section-8 housing developments, I sold marijuana, I had illicit relationships, and now I am an educated author, who helps organizations increase their performance through effective leadership and deliver more desirable results. Glory to God! I don't care if you're wearing your white wig, black robe and holding your gavel. Judge away! Or you can celebrate the fact I didn't throw my life away in jail after robbing your home or were murdered.

Another attribute of a trustworthy person is resourcefulness. Often, people who aren't resourceful quit. They quit on themselves and their efforts. Not all of them, but often (from my experience). Out-the-box thinking and that driven attitude to find away, is attractive to a leader. That g.r.i.t. and determination is necessary to be a great follower. Grit is in the form of an acronym because I gave it one (Get Ready It's Tough). That is from my leadership development program, *Leading from the Roots: 11 Characteristics of a Great Leader*. Leadership and followship, both require grit and it's tough. So, is quitting on yourself. So, you might as well tough it out and see it through.

The Eagle Fly's West at Dawn

The United States government uses a code name for the President of the United States, to protect him. This code name is only available on a 'needs to know' basis. They use this method of safety because they understand the foundational principle of it: Discretion. In order for you to be a great follower, you must be discreet. Discretion in a great follower is important. Discretion builds trust. I know I personally trust people who are more discreet than loud and drawing attention to themselves. Discretion says you can hang with the big boys/girls at the top. Where colossal problems are discussed. I can also trust for you to carry yourself with dignity and professionalism.

A great way to find out if someone is discreet, is to simply look at their social media. Just read 10 posts, you'll see it right away. They'll share their personal problems, they'll air out their relationship issues, they have to post every single thing they're doing. That is the opposite of discretion. Ironically, I have found that most social media influencers who record their entire life are very much discreet. It could be that they air everything else out and they want to keep something to themselves. Discretion makes your life easier. Discretion limits opinions in your life, it builds trust and relationships, it strengthens your value and makes you rare. The reason leaders are so selective about who they mentor is because of things like discretion.

Another benefit of discretion is control. Discretion controls the flow of communication for the greater good of the team. You ever heard the term; "Running your mouth"? That comes from not being discreet. Like announcing a leadership change too soon, causing chaos, confusion, and fear amongst the team. Or announcing a team gathering before the leader was ready to announce it. Discretion is a control tool. You want to shut up outside opinions by controlling what they know? Be discreet. You want to control what your kids know about your next family trip? Be discreet. You want to keep fascinated by your "secret life" because you didn't share your entire story with them? Be discreet. Keep control through discretion.

I remember I went to a company Christmas party one year (for the sake of discretion, I am going to change the industry in which I worked), and one of the Executive Assistants were drunk. She ran around the Christmas party airing out one of the executives dirty laundry. She was telling everyone that she orders flowers for so many different women, every week. With the same message in the card, "I love you and miss you". Well, everyone began to naturally believe this doctor was having affairs left and right. What she didn't know is that the doctor wasn't having affairs, he was reminding his sisters that he loved them and missed them. He hadn't seen his sisters in years and just missed them. Needless to say, this person wasn't a great follower. She wasn't even a great teammate.

To jeopardize and sabotage the leaders influence with his team because you lack discretion is embarrassing and cancerous to a team. I was stunned that she did that. What I came to find out is that she was drunk as a skunk. People who are discreet avoid scenarios like this. They understand that liquor can impact your brain. The decisions you would normally make are no longer as obvious. They are harder to make or even to decipher. If you are discreet in nature, you're probably sweating right now. Reading all these horror examples of talking too damn much. People generally dislike how discreet I am. And I understand why. The rest of the world is not like that, they're not used to it. They may not even be like that. That's your prerogative. Not mine. That's ok. We can be different. You'll just have to adapt and adjust to get yourself comfortable. Or not.

One way to identify a discreet person is in their question asking. You will find that discreet people do not asking probing, personal questions. They avoid it like the plague. They think they are being highly offensive and intrusive. Because to them, that is what that would feel like. Discreet people don't ask about your finances, personal problems, or your gossip of any sort. They understand that boundary and they respect it. I love people like that. I'm not hiding anything; I just don't feel comfortable opening up. That goes for family too at times. It's not personal. Just a comfort thing. I am sure there is a psychologist that could tell me what this is called. Either way, it is who I am. Discretion is not a bad thing. It's healthy and the path of least stress.

I Couldn't Do this Without You

As a leader of a team, it has always been important to me that my staff understands their assignment. Or, in other words, understands their role. Some people might say "operating within your sandbox". In order for you to be a great follower, you must be a team player. After all, the success of an organization or team is within its players/staff. Leaders cannot do their role without them. Period. Now, understanding your role is just a piece of being a team player. Not only do you need to understand your role and respect the boundaries of your position, but you must also be open to collaboration.

When working collaboratively, you are subject to other ideas and opinions that may differ from yours. I actually welcome that. Why? Because I don't always have the best solution. Or sometimes people on my team have been thinking about this problem and brainstorming longer than I have, and they have a fantastic solution or idea. As someone who is on this collaborative team, you need to be open to hearing other people out, before pushing your idea as the end all, be all. When listening to yourself or others, search for compromises and be respectful to others you are to collaborate with. Don't be married to your idea until you have complete buy-in. Then you go all in.

Another trait of a great follower who is a team player is accountability. We talked about this earlier. But your actions or lack thereof; impacts more than you when you are on a team. Let me give you an example. Kyrie Irving (as I write this book) is the starting all-star point guard for the *Brooklyn Nets* NBA Basketball franchise. When the State of New York implemented a vaccine mandate for athletes in their state to play home games, Kyrie took a stance and said he was not getting vaccinated. Whether his belief was right or wrong, is not what I am talking about here. What I want to mention is that he missed 53 games out of 82 that season. He was allowed to play away games in states that did not have a vaccine mandate. At playoffs time, NY removed their vaccine mandate and Kyrie Irving was allowed to play home games in the playoffs. Unfortunately, for the Brooklyn Nets, they were eliminated from playoff contention.

Now, Kyrie was shredded by sports media for not getting vaccinated – watching his team lose games and lowering their playoff rank. The impact of Kyrie Irving not getting vaccinated was detrimental to the team and setting them up for a sweet position in the playoffs. It also created some hostility in the locker room. His actions had an impact on the entire team. One thing I will acknowledge is Kyrie was accountable to his lack of action towards getting vaccinated.

Being accountable is critical to your team and yourself as a great follower. Being accountable helps you learn from your errors and earn respect from your team. If you can't learn to say, "I screwed up", no one is going to trust you with anything big. No one is going to expect great things from you. They can't because you aren't accountable.

Most people have watched Bambi or have heard the saying; "If you don't have nothing nice to say, don't say anything at all". In the marketplace, it goes slightly different, "If you don't have anything positive to say, don't say anything at all". What I am not referring to hear is not speaking up when there's a problem. I am referring to having a problem for every solution. When you are on a team and everyone is working collectively to resolve issues, the last thing people want to hear is a negative attitude. Just shhhh! Unless you have something significantly better to communicate. Negativity is useless energy. What does it really accomplish? At least positivity and optimism have a proven, productive track record.

You don't have to understand the entire solution right away, to be positive about it. I have been part of corporate decisions that I was in a complete fog about for a while before I understood the "how", but you better bet your ass I was going to be supportive. Why would I get in the way of progress because someone peed in my *Wheaties* that morning? You owe it to yourself and your team to be a positive, contributing member of it.

Commitment is a funny thing. Some people measure their commitment based on someone else's. For instance, in my early years of attending church. I would sometimes get offended by what some staffer at the church said. At that point I would just check out mentally, but I was serving on a team. Then a pastor reminded me that the church is ran by humans. People who make mistakes. Of course, I judged everyone else by their actions, but wanted to be judged by my intentions (which is not how life works at all). To this day, there are people who offended me in church. I chalk it up to their own personal issues and keep it moving. A healthy, great follower understands that commitment is internal and controlled by them. When you commit to a team, you must fully invest. Go all in, like you are playing poker and your hand can't lose. You never know who you may inspire by your commitment to your team and leader.

So, how do you do all this? Be available to your team. Offer assistance and keep an eye out for someone who may look or seem overwhelmed. Can you lighten their load? Can you be an ear to possibly vent to? Can you be a positive, encouraging member of the team? If you are going to do that, be an active listener. Listen to understand, ask questions, thoughtfully respond. Another way to show your commitment is to communicate. Keep your leader or team updated on your progress with a project or task you've been assigned. Consistent communication let's everyone stop and making sure you are all working towards the same goal.

Last, but certainly not least, celebrate! Everyone and every small victory! A team member who knows how to celebrate the little things understands the big picture of progress. Being a great follower is work! It is not natural to be this way. Life keeps moving. In our darkest days, hardest seasons, the sun rises and sets – consistently. You sometimes wish it would just pause for a moment. But it doesn't. Ever. So, keeping that positivity and encouragement can be a challenge at times. Celebrating others when you are in a tough season in your life or career is hard to do. Do it anyways. When you don't feel like it, push through the challenges. Tell yourself that you are going to be a positive light for your leader and team. Your leader cannot do this without you. Be an armor-bearer as my friend Larry Ward would say. Protect your leader!

If you want to know where you can get better within this characteristic of commitment, ask a colleague you trust or your leader. Don't assume you have this nailed down. If your leader, flips the question back to you, give them your honest opinion of yourself. They may agree with you or be surprised to hear of what you do that they are unaware of. Be vulnerable and open to feedback. Don't get your feelings hurt if you hear something you didn't want to hear. Try to understand where your leader or colleague is coming from. Eat the meat and leave the bones! Take what is valuable and disregard what isn't. Remember, a team is not a group of people who work together, they are a group of people who trust each other.

You Don't Have to Be a Keynote

When I get up on a stage to keynote, a lot of people ask me, "How do you do that with no fear?" I always give the same reasons: I have prepared for this for a while and no one knows when I went off script of messed up, but me. I have had many occasions where someone was so kind to me to call me a great communicator. Now, every channel of communication is not on stage. As a matter of fact, most communication is not on stage. As a great follower, you may never get a chance to be on a stage. And that is ok. But, in order for you to be a great follower, you must be a communicator.

Communication starts at the ears, not the mouth. Listening is a vital piece of communication. You cannot genuinely listen to someone while you are preparing your response. Sometimes we can get so wrapped up in our response, we neglect to listen. When your leader is speaking, you should be listening. I really don't know any other way to put that. You have two ears and one mouth for a reason. When you are a great follower, communication will help you sustain that. Communication helps you both personally and professionally. Communication allows for harvesting meaningful relationships, genuine understanding, and can increase production. Ask any successful salesperson if communication is critical. Ask any Pastor, Lawyer, Judge, Spouse or Teacher. Communication (listening then responding) is an anchor in any relationship.

There is an increasing number of studies that tie employee satisfaction to empathy. They are looking for empathetic leaders. Leaders who have listened and said, "I'll help". You cannot gain empathy without first listening. Now, some of you may be reading this and thinking "he is really focusing on listening when talking about communication". That is because it's where communication starts! It doesn't start at you opening your mouth. Letting your leader know you care about what they are saying is important to becoming a great follower. Now, let's switch gears to the part of communication that requires the use of your mouth.

Let's start with confidence. If you are not confident in what is about to come out of your mouth, don't say it. The last impression you want to give to your leader is that you lack confidence. Confidence grows your credibility. When speaking, take moments to pause. People who ramble (especially at a fast pace) generally come off as nervous. Don't be. You know what you want to say because you have prepared for it. The audience is listening because they believe you to be prepared and confident, prove it to them.

Not only is confidence important, but so is being friendly. Speaking and writing in a friendly tone makes people want to communicate with you more. They like talking to you or reading your emails. A bunch of exclamation marks and question marks make you look like you're emotionally unintelligent. When you are speaking to someone, use their name several times in the conversation. Remind them you see them as a person not a resource. Another key attribute of a great follower who is a great communicator is being observant. This is where we are focusing on non-verbal communication cues. What is your body language telling someone? Are you slouching? Are you shifty? Is your back turned to them? Is your head in your phone? Are you not making eye contact? All these are terrible messages you are sending with your body language to your leader or anyone for that matter.

If you aren't looking at me when talking to me, what you have to say must not be important. If you are slouching, you must be content with whatever the outcome is in what you're talking about. If you are shifty, you must be nervous. If your head is in your phone, I am not listening to you. Some of these assumptions could be way off the mark, but I promise, this is what your leader and colleagues are thinking about. So, straighten up, look them in the eyes, put your phone away and on silent, stay in place and definitely be facing them.

Appreciation goes a long way. When speaking with someone, show them appreciation for their time and ear. Providing a positive, verbal reinforcement helps generate future interactions with that person. "Can I have a moment of your time?" Sure! Why? Because the last interaction was so pleasant, I actually enjoy communicating with you. Or, "Nope!" Why? Because you disrespected me and my time the last time we spoke. I will not waste my time with you. Harsh, but very much a reality. It's like when trying to give advice to someone who is complaining to you about something. Yet, they have an excuse for everything you throw at them. Fine, I am done. It's too exhausting and you're messing up my vibe.

Ok, these next two attributes are very important. First, be organized! When communicating, if you are all over the place, I cannot follow your conversation. You will lose me so fast. I need this conversation to flow. Have you ever spoke to someone who jumps from one thing to another without a single transitional statement? It is so hard to shift gears with them. It's like driving a stick shift car without a clutch. Stay on track and don't go on some rabbit trail. You will lose your audience and they will lose interest in the important message you are trying to share.

Secondly, use good judgment. This has multiple layers. First, use good judgment on your audience. Everyone doesn't need to know everything. I don't tell everyone my dreams and goals; some won't understand it. I am also giving them the impression that they can speak on it. I don't want that. Make sure who you are communicating to is the correct audience for the message. Also, use good judgment on the means of communication. Is this more of a phone call, face-to-face or an email? The method in which you communicate matters. Also use good judgment on the timing. Your leader just expressed how your department is over budget and you set a meeting to talk about a raise? Probably not the ideal time for that conversation. You don't want your message lost in translation due to timing.

Set yourself up for success by zeroing in on this characteristic of communication and the attributes I have outlined. It will help you become a great communicator.

Are We There Yet?

In 1971, Carly Simon wrote a hit song titled; "Anticipation". Part of the lyrics said, "Anticipation, it's making me wait, keeping me awake". When kids anticipate something, it is generally for their own selfish reasons. Like on a road trip and they ask, "are we there yet?" The sarcastic dad in me wants to reply, "have we stopped?" But that isn't the greatest response. Generally, when we talk about anticipation in the marketplace, we talk about leaders. Anticipating hurdles and obstacles for the team or organization. But I believe it starts before a leadership role. I believe it starts as a follower. In order for you to be a great follower, you must learn to anticipate.

Anticipation is an invaluable asset of a great follower. If you can anticipate the needs of your leader, you can make their lives easier. You are a blessing to them. Your leader has a big meeting coming up, what can you do to help set them up for success? Ok, she is going to need me to step up here and cover "x" while she's gone. He is going to need this report from me before he leaves. Whatever the need you are filling, it is important. Looking ahead is not a normal practice for many. But it is a damn good one. Imagine being the leader preparing for a big business trip or meeting, you start to realize things that you need and one of your great followers tells you they took care of it already. It's a weight off your shoulders and you have one less thing to worry about. Imagine you coming home for work and your kids have already showered and laid their clothes out for school tomorrow. Or your spouse takes your car and fills up your gas tank because they noticed you were close to empty. Anticipation is amazing!

There is a reason there is increased security in Time Square on New Year's Eve. It's because the city is anticipating a large crowd that could get rowdy. They want reinforcements to control the gathering. Without anticipation, our military and country would be incredibly vulnerable to attacks. Without anticipation our President is vulnerable to being attacked. Without anticipation your organization is vulnerable to loss and failure. As a business owner, you must anticipate obstacles you may face. That is why businesses do a S.W.O.T. analysis (Strengths, Weaknesses, Opportunities and Threats). Without that, you are surely going to make your journey much harder than it needs to be.

Anticipation allows you to limit surprises. Anticipation can also be a very positive thing. If you are going to propose to someone and you are certain they are going to say 'yes', anticipation can be fun! If you are about to fulfill a bucket list item, anticipation can be exciting. Anticipation is an emotional experience. Enjoy that journey! As a great follower, anticipation is a value-add. Your leader can trust that you have thought this all the way through. Whatever "this" is. All it takes is one critical moment of anticipation to build trust. Consistent anticipation sustains it. As a leader, if I do not have someone, I can count on to help me anticipate, I am like Carly Simon…it's keeping me awake.

Kids anticipate the arrival to, let's say *Disneyland*. They are excited to go to the "*happiest place on earth!*" And they should be! Anticipation can be fun. Especially if your anticipation cleared a path for you or your leader. So, as a great follower, anticipate something. If it's not for your leader, do it for you! Or your family! Anticipate your next promotion. Anticipate your next family vacation. With anticipation comes action. You don't just receive a promotion, you don't just show up at a family vacation destination, you must put work in! Anticipation to me is a verb. So, ask yourself; "What can I anticipate, right now?" Then ask yourself; "What have I done to help manifest that, or avoid it?"

Conclusion

My hope is that this book has inspired you and has given you a different perspective on being a follower. The world needs followers. Leaders need followers. There is nothing wrong with being a great follower. Whatever path you choose, please choose to be great. The world needs you. YOU! Not another version of someone else. You were specifically and uniquely designed for a purpose. When you tap into that purpose, you will find fulfillment and happiness. It could very well be that your purpose is to be a great follower. Don't let it pass you by due to your ego or the world's view of being a follower. If you work for an organization, give them your all. Commit and be excellent. Do everything you possibly can to excel. If that doesn't work out as "anticipated" that is ok! It's not over and they do not dictate your purpose.

When you see your leader succeed, smile, and know that you helped them get there. You played a pivotal role in their success. To whoever I lead or have led, I want to thank you from the bottom of my heart for your contributions to my success. I could not and did not do it without you. You are my anchors and I love you all. I am in complete gratitude of those I have led that I have had to terminate employment (you taught me lessons – it wasn't personal, I promise), of those that deserved to be terminated but I acted too slow and for those who were my peace in tough seasons. You all have added unique value in my life and I am forever grateful.

To the leaders who have guided me to this point, thank you!!!!! For better or worse, it was all a lesson. To my family, I love you (most of you – just kidding). To all the leaders I have watched fail publicly, it wasn't in vain, I learned a lot. For those who are scared to jump into leadership or followship, don't be! Both are hard and both require work – but you got this!!! Stick to the script!

www.ingramcontent.com/pod-product-compliance
Lightning Source LLC
Chambersburg PA
CBHW051539240526

45465CB00028B/1558